UP CLOSE

Rainforest

PAUL HARRISON

W

Reprinted in 2012
This paperback edition published in 2011 by Franklin Watts

Copyright © 2009 Arcturus Publishing Limited

Franklin Watts
338 Euston Road
London NW1 3BH

Franklin Watts Australia
Level 17/207 Kent Street
Sydney, NSW 2000

Author: Paul Harrison
Editor (new edition): Fiona Tulloch
Designers (new edition): Trevor Cook, Sally Henry

Picture credits: FLPA: front cover, title page, 6, 7, 11 bottom, 15 top and back cover, 19 bottom; Jungle Photos: 18 top; Nature Picture Library: 5 top, 9 bottom, 10 top, 14 bottom, 20 top, 21 top and bottom; NHPA: 4 bottom, 11 top, 15 bottom, 16, 17 top; Still Pictures: 12 top, 17 bottom, 18 bottom, 19 top, 20 bottom.

A CIP catalogue record for this book is available from the British Library

Dewey number: 578.7'34

ISBN: 978-1-4451-0860-5
SL000955EN

Printed in China

Franklin Watts is a division of Hachette Children's Books, an Hachette UK Company
www.hachette.co.uk

Supplier 03, Date 0412, Print Run 1818

Contents

What Is a Rainforest?

There are *tropical* rainforests all round the *equator*, in Africa, Central and South America, Asia and Australia.

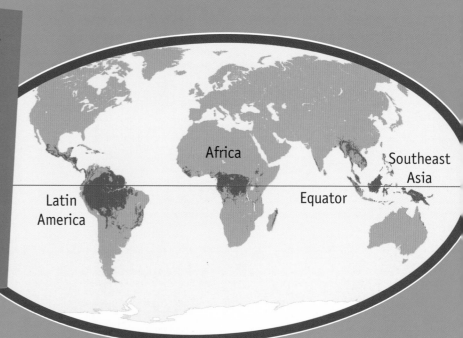

Africa

Latin America

Equator

Southeast Asia

NOT ALL THE SAME

Most rainforests are in the lowlands where it's warm and wet. The forests on higher ground are called cloud forests, because they're often surrounded by clouds. Away from the equator, there are *monsoon* or moist forests.

TALL STOREYS

The forest has four levels. The forest floor is the lowest. Larger animals are found there.

The next level up is called the understorey. Above this is the canopy, which is an umbrella-like cover formed by the leafy branches.

At the top level, the tallest trees in the forest rise up through the canopy.

CROWDED HOUSE

Half the world's plants and animals live in the rainforests, which cover only 6 per cent of the Earth's surface.

There are probably lots of new *species* of plants and animals in the rainforest, just waiting to be discovered!

The South American rainforest of the Amazon and the Central American tropical forest together have the widest range of animals anywhere in the world.

Sloths move about so little that plants and *algae* can grow on them!

NO HIDING PLACE

Even animals as big as monkeys aren't safe when the fearsome harpy eagle swoops down on the tree tops of the Central American forest.

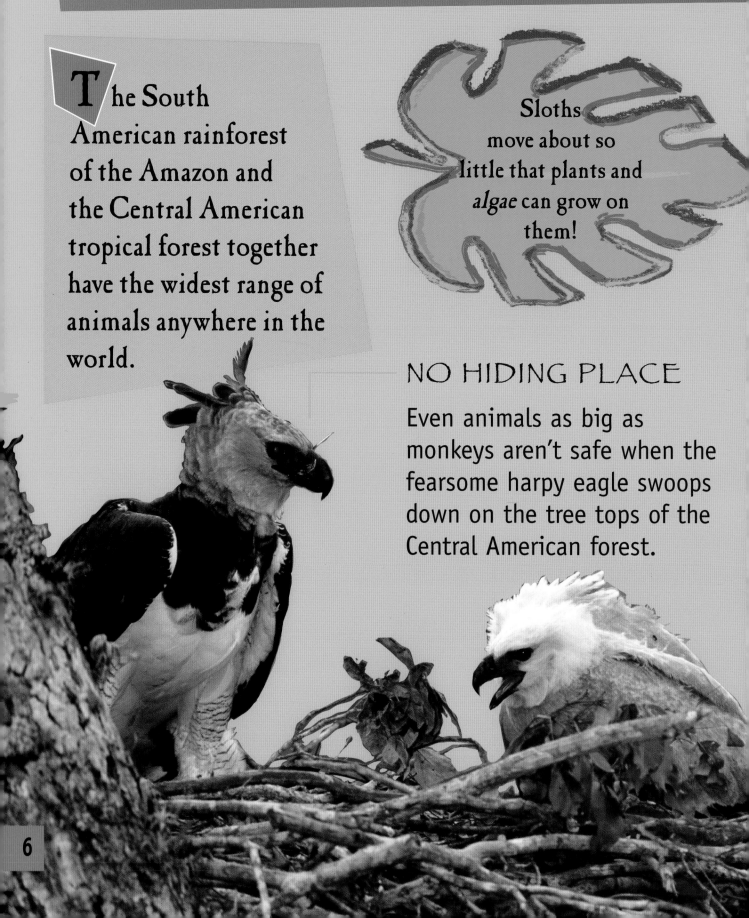

American Rainforest

THE BEAR FACTS

The children's book character Paddington Bear was based on the spectacled bear, South America's only type of bear. The real animal eats fruit, nuts, plants and small animals, not marmalade sandwiches like Paddington!

TOUCAN PLAY

Toucans are known for their enormous, colourful beaks. They use this light and strong beak for reaching fruit. It's also very useful for frightening off enemies.

The giant anteater can eat up to 30,000 ants and termites every day.

HUMMING ALONG

The wings of the hummingbird, from South America, beat 80 times per second in normal flight.

A RIVER RUNS THROUGH IT

The Amazon rainforest is named after the mighty Amazon river, it flows nearly 6,300 kilometres, from the Andes mountains to the Atlantic ocean. It's the world's largest river by the volume of water. It's also home to thousands of species of animals, including river dolphins, turtles, fearsome piranha fish and anacondas.

DEADLY COLOURS

The poison dart frog defends itself by making poison ooze from its skin. It's deadly enough to kill a monkey-sized animal. Amerindians use the poison on the tips of their blow pipe darts for hunting. The general rule in the rainforest is if it's colourful, it's dangerous!

The African Rainforest

Africa has the second largest area of rainforest after the Amazon. It is spread over many countries.

JUNGLE ARMY

One of the smallest *predators* in the forest is also among the fiercest. The driver ant moves in swarms of millions, and can eat goats, cows and even elephants!

Gorillas sleep in nests above the ground. They build a new one every night.

GENTLE GIANT

Once wrongly thought of as a violent creature, the gorilla is an intelligent and gentle animal. It lives in groups called troops, each led by a dominant male called a silverback, after the grey hairs on his back.

NOT SO PRETTY POLLY

The grey parrot is not colourful, but it can really talk! Trade in these birds has made them an endangered species. *Poachers* are still catching them, though.

TASTY

Thousands of fruits and edible plants grow in the rainforest. In Africa, coffee, yams, bananas and palm oil are just a few of the foodstuffs produced.

LITTLE AND LARGE

The African rainforest is very dense and difficult to study. Scientists only recently realised that the jungle elephant is a different species from its larger relative which lives on the African *savannah*.

The elephant's tusks are a kind of teeth. They are used for feeding and as weapons.

WELL SPOTTED!

The purpose of the leopard's distinctive spotted pattern is *camouflage*. It works as well in the dappled shade of the rainforest as on grasslands, mountains and deserts.

The Asian Rainforest

There's a huge variety of plants and animals in this rainforest, which stretches from India to New Guinea.

OLD MAN

The orang-utan is often called the old man of the forest. He's a shy and intelligent animal and closely related to man. He spends most of his time above ground and is rarely seen. His long, powerful arms are great for swinging through the trees.

STINKER

The world's largest flower is the rafflesia. It is found in the jungles of Borneo. It can measure up to 1 metre across. Not recommended for the garden at home – it stinks of rotting meat!

PASSENGERS

Plants like rafflesia are parasites – they get their nourishment directly from other plants. Other plants, called epiphytes, use their neighbours as a platform to get closer to the light.

15

The Australian Rainforest

Australia's rainforests are a long way from all the others. There are some surprising animals and plants living there.

HOPPING ALONG

There are 11 species of tree kangaroo. Some are so well adapted to life in the trees that they find it difficult to move around on the ground.

Tree kangaroos and possums are both marsupials, which means they carry their young in pouches on their fronts.

NIGHT CRAWLERS

The green ringtail possum spends most of its time above the ground. Like many rainforest animals, it is active at night (nocturnal). This means it has fewer predators to worry about. During the day it sleeps in the branches, curled in a tight ball.

FEELING BLUE

Butterflies are some of the most colourful insects in the Australian rainforest. The Ulysses butterfly is one of the most spectacular. It is also known as the mountain blue. It's easy to spot – it's over 24 centimetres across and bright blue.

Rainforest People

A s well as many plants and animals, about 50 million people live in the world's rainforests. Around 1000 different tribes have learned how to live in this difficult environment.

ON THE MOVE

Many rainforest people, like this member of the Huli tribe from Papua New Guinea, don't farm animals or cultivate plants. They have to move to where food can be found.

EXTREME FARMING

Tribes like the Yanomamo of Brazil clear fields in the rainforest by chopping down the understorey. They grow food there. After a year or two the exhausted ground is abandoned to be reseeded by the jungle.

FOUND IN THE FOREST

All the materials you need to live can be found in the forest! This woman from the Mbuti tribe in Zaire is making a house from branches and leaves. It will only be used until the tribe moves on to a new place.

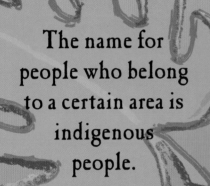

The name for people who belong to a certain area is indigenous people.

A DISAPPEARING HOME

As the resources of the rainforest get taken away, many tribes have lost much of their forest home. Some of the tribes, and many other people in the world, have protested and now the future looks brighter for at least some parts of the forests.

Hotting Up

I f the clearing of the rainforests goes on at the current rate, they will be totally wiped out within 50 years. That's bad for everyone! Here's why …

CARBON COPY

When trees are cut down, they give off a lot of carbon dioxide. This adds to global warming. Rainforests absorb carbon dioxide – but they absorb less as they get smaller.

USEFUL PLANTS

Many drugs we use today come from plants found in the rain forest. The more the rainforests are cleared, the fewer of these plants can be found.

FOOD FOR THOUGHT

In some places in Africa, dead rainforest animals of many kinds – bush meat – have become a key part of people's diets.
Sadly, this is pushing some species close to extinction.

Some environmentalists estimate that an area of rainforest the size of a football field is cleared every second!

TIMBER

Huge areas of rainforest have been cut down to supply timber. The cleared soil is often shallow, low in *fertility*, and easily washed away by rains.

Glossary

Algae
Primitive plant which is often green, but without stems or leaves

Camouflage
Hide something by making it look like something else

Equator
The imaginary line which runs around the centre of the earth

Fertility
Having the things in a soil which help plants to grow

Monsoon
The season when it rains a lot

especially in Asian countries

Poachers
People who hunt animals illegally

Predator
An animal that kills and eats other animals

Savannah
Large areas of flat grassland in warm regions of the world

Species
A group of similar plants or animals

Tropical
The hottest part of the world where the rainforests are

Further Reading

Rainforest
Helen Sharman, Dorling Kindersley (Eye Wonder series), 2004

Life in the Rainforest
Kathryn Senior, Book House (What On Earth series, 2006

Journey into the Rainforest
Tim Knight, Oxford University Press, 2001

Rainforest
DK Children (Revealed series), 2004

Rainforest Animals
Stephen Savage, Wayland (Focus On Habitats series), 2006

Rainforests
Peter Riley, Scholastic (Hot Topics series), 2008

Index